The Art of
Making Silk

Rob Waring, *Series Editor*

NATIONAL
GEOGRAPHIC
L E A R N I N G

Australia · Brazil · Mexico · Singapore · United Kingdom · United States

Words to Know

This story is set in Europe, in the country of Italy. It happens in the city of Florence [flɔrəns].

A **Fabric Making.** Read the sentences. Label the items in the picture with the underlined words.

A weaver is a person who makes cloth on a machine.
A loom is a machine with which cloth is made.
Fabric is a type of cloth or material.
A thread is a long, thin piece of cotton, wool, etc. that is used for sewing.

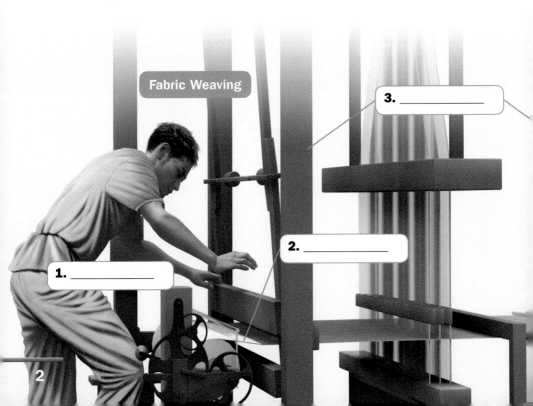

Fabric Weaving

1. _____
2. _____
3. _____

B **A Silk Factory.** Read the paragraph. Then match each word with the correct definition.

This story is about a traditional silk factory in Florence, Italy. The highly skilled craftsmen there produce high-quality silk cloth on ancient machines. The beautiful silk fabrics are often used as draperies for the windows of houses, or for furniture upholstery. The factory is one of the few places left that makes these handwoven designs.

1. silk _____

2. craftsman _____

3. draperies _____

4. upholstery _____

5. handwoven _____

a. long pieces of material which hang down to cover something

b. the material that covers chairs and other types of seats

c. made by hand; not made by a machine

d. a special type of cloth which is light and smooth

e. a specially trained person who makes something, usually with the hands

4. _____

The ancient city of Florence changes very slowly. Its narrow stone streets are very much the same as they were when the famous **Medici family**[1] ruled it more than 500 years ago. The city has seen a number of important historical events over the years: the **Renaissance**,[2] the Industrial Revolution, and the World Wars. These events have had an effect on the city, but at one factory the ways of the past are still practiced. This factory is the ***Antico Setificio Fiorentino***,[3] or the Antique Silk Factory of Florence.

---

[1] **the Medici family:** a very powerful family in Florence from the 12th to 17th centuries
[2] **the Renaissance:** a cultural movement that took place from the 14th through the 17th centuries, beginning in Italy and later spreading to the rest of Europe
[3] ***Antico Setificio Fiorentino:*** [æntikoʊ sɛtəfitʃoʊ fiɔrɛntinoʊ]

🎧 **CD 2, Track 09**

Behind the leaf-covered walls of the traditional silk factory, or *Setificio*, lies the main area of the factory. In it, the continuous noise of incredibly old mechanical looms brings one back to the past. The noisy looms in this section are from the 1800s and they create some of the world's finest silk fabrics for draperies and upholstery. However, while these machines may be old, at this factory they are actually the 'new' machines. In another part of the factory, one can find the real pieces of history—looms that have been around for centuries!

Scan for Information

Scan Pages 9 to 10 to answer the questions:

1. How old are the oldest looms at the *Setificio* factory?

2. How many companies in Italy still weave silk by hand?

3. What are two differences between industrially produced silk and handmade silk?

Stefano **Benelli**[4] is one of the craftsmen at the factory. He is a weaver who makes the silk fabric that machines alone cannot create. He stands over a huge loom and works slowly and carefully, weaving one thread at a time. Above him, there are special paper cards that carry the designs for complicated patterns. As Benelli weaves, the information on these cards helps to create a design in the silk.

These looms were built in 1780, and they apply the same principles of weaving that were used for hundreds of years before that. Sabine Pretsch, the factory's director, talks about the tradition of making silk at the *Setificio*. She explains that although they use old machines, the company is still very creative. "Everything is done like it was done in the ancient time," she says and then adds, "We continue to [have] an **evolution**.[5] Continuously, we invent. We create continuously by using the old looms."

───────────────────────

[4] **Benelli:** [bənɛli]
[5] **evolution:** a period of development through a number of stages

After the Second World War ended in 1945, other Italian silk **manufacturers**[6] threw away their slower hand looms. That left the *Setificio* alone in the handmade silk industry. It is now the only factory in Italy that still uses hand looms in a large-scale silk manufacturing process.

Is all of the hard work involved with making silk by hand worth it? Many people seem to think so. There's certainly a big difference between industrially produced silk and handwoven silk. Industrially produced silk usually has 3,000 to 4,000 threads running in one direction on a full piece of fabric. The silk produced on the old hand looms has 12,000 threads in the same amount of space. That's up to four times the number of threads that are used! The number of threads used in the silk-making process affects the quality of the silk in a number of ways, including how it looks and how it feels.

---

[6]**manufacturer:** a company that produces goods in large amounts

One important quality of the silk that is affected by weaving style is the strength. There are so many threads used in handmade silk that it is very strong. Another important quality that is affected is the color. With handweaving, the threads of the silk don't **twist**,[7] so they show the full range of color and are more beautiful. As she touches the beautiful material, Sabine Pretsch explains that handweaving brings out a red color and a beautiful softened effect in the fabric. She then explains that the color changes depending on the light.

Believe it or not, the sound of handmade silk is different, too! Pretsch explains that handwoven silk makes a special noise and holds whatever shape it is formed to very well. This doesn't happen with machine-made silks. They don't have the beautiful red color, the special sounds of handmade silk, and they don't hold their shape as well either.

---

[7]**twist:** turn, usually repeatedly; wrap around one another

Even before the weaving begins, the silk threads that are used to weave are treated specially. First, natural silk is processed on machines that are 150 years old, nearly as old as the hand looms. These machines turn natural silk pieces into very fine thread. Then, the threads are prepared according to how they will be used. The threads that will be used for the wide part of the fabric are called the weft. Weft threads are very carefully placed on a **bobbin**[8] so that the threads are not twisted. The threads that will be used for the warp, or the long part of the fabric, are gathered together to create long groups of thread. Again, the craftsmen are very careful not to twist the thread to ensure the quality of the fabric.

[8]**bobbin:** a small piece of wood or plastic on which thread is stored

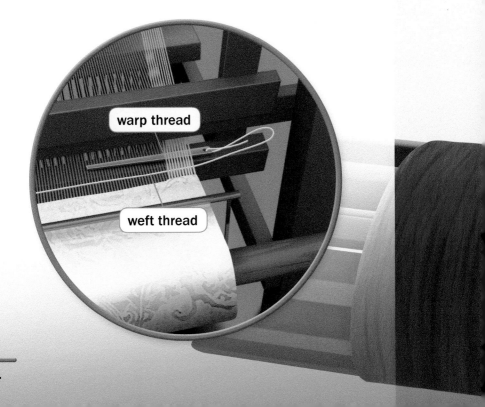

bobbin

Warp and weft threads are prepared differently.

In the end, very high quality silk fabrics are produced with this complicated process. In addition, all of the fabrics that are made at the *Setificio* are special—they can't be found in stores or anywhere else. Every piece of cloth is **custom-made**.[9]

Of course, the work required to make such luxurious cloth takes time and is very difficult. Weaving by hand on a loom is hard, repetitive work—the weaver has to do the same thing many times. But what may seem like difficult and boring work to some people is enjoyable to a craftsman like Benelli. He says that he doesn't mind the repetitive work at all. As he points to his head he says with a smile, "The mind is okay. [It's not] **stressful!**"[10]

---

[9]**custom-made:** made especially for one person or purpose
[10]**stressful:** causing worry or anxiety

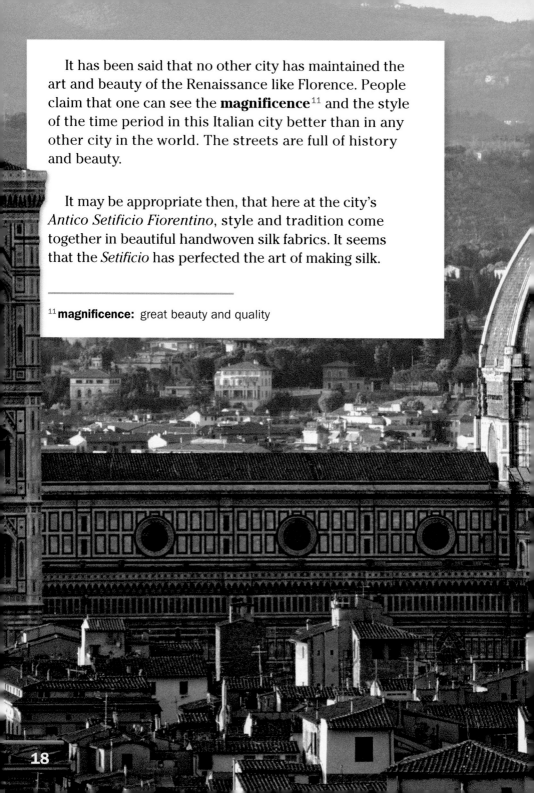

It has been said that no other city has maintained the art and beauty of the Renaissance like Florence. People claim that one can see the **magnificence**[11] and the style of the time period in this Italian city better than in any other city in the world. The streets are full of history and beauty.

It may be appropriate then, that here at the city's *Antico Setificio Fiorentino*, style and tradition come together in beautiful handwoven silk fabrics. It seems that the *Setificio* has perfected the art of making silk.

---

[11] **magnificence:** great beauty and quality

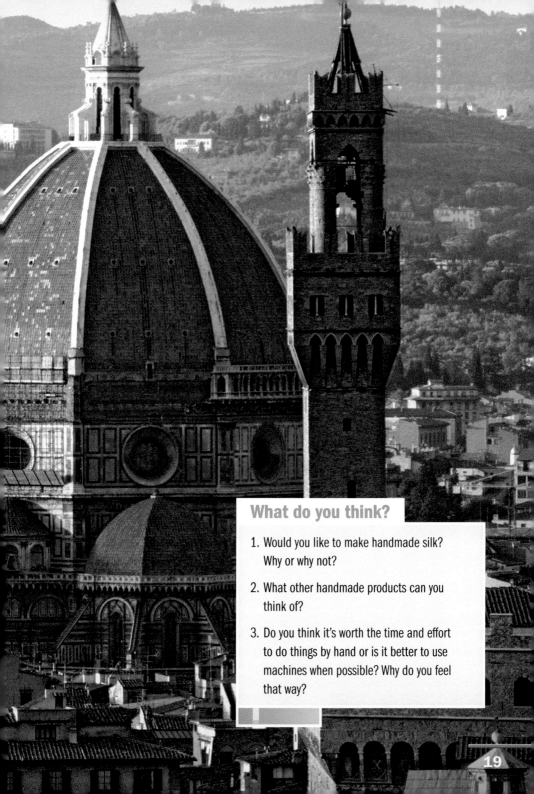

What do you think?

1. Would you like to make handmade silk? Why or why not?

2. What other handmade products can you think of?

3. Do you think it's worth the time and effort to do things by hand or is it better to use machines when possible? Why do you feel that way?

After You Read

1. Florence is a city _____ a great history.
   A. and
   B. with
   C. of
   D. about

2. How does the silk factory stay connected to the past?
   A. The looms inside are the same as centuries before.
   B. The weavers tell stories from a long time ago.
   C. The equipment is modern, but the building is old.
   D. The factory only sells ancient Medici silk.

3. What is the meaning of the word 'complicated' in paragraph 1 on page 9?
   A. strange
   B. interesting
   C. complex
   D. pretty

4. What view about the factory is expressed by Sabine Pretsch on page 9?
   A. The silk made there is the best in the world.
   B. The workers there are very hard-working.
   C. The machines are the reason for its success.
   D. The design ideas there are always changing.

5. What does the writer probably think about handmade silk?
   A. The quality is excellent.
   B. The work is quick and simple.
   C. There are too many threads.
   D. The loom often breaks.

6. How do hand looms show more color in the silk?
   A. by using thread on the looms
   B. by using an experienced weaver
   C. by not twisting the threads
   D. by strengthing the fabric

7. In paragraph 1 on page 13, what is 'it' referring to?
  A. the fabric
  B. a loom
  C. thread
  D. the *Setificio*

8. What's a good heading for paragraph 2 on page 13?
  A. Only Machines Make Red
  B. Listen and Discover Quality
  C. Handmade Silk Loses Shape
  D. Noisy Silk Doesn't Sell

9. Which is NOT involved in making and preparing silk thread?
  A. organizing threads by use
  B. placing weft threads on a bobbin
  C. gathering threads for the warp
  D. twisting the threads for use

10. Every piece of cloth from the *Setificio* is _____.
  A. long and difficult
  B. usual
  C. rare
  D. available at any store

11. What word on page 18 means 'kept'?
  A. full
  B. perfected
  C. claim
  D. maintained

12. The purpose of page 18 is to show that:
  A. Florence is the most popular city in Italy.
  B. *Setificio* silk is the highest quality in the world.
  C. Florence's ancient traditions can be experienced at *Setificio*.
  D. Handwoven Italian silk is perfect.

Class: Science

Teacher: Mr. Park

Assignment: Write a short report about an insect.

The Amazing Silkworm
by Koby Wenger

Silk is produced by the caterpillar called *Bombyx Mori*. The name more commonly used for this caterpillar is 'silkworm.' The silkworm has very limited eating habits; it only eats leaves from a single type of plant—the Mulberry tree. In fact, *Bombyx Mori* is Latin for 'silkworm of the Mulberry tree.' This unusual animal begins life as a tiny egg that is only a little bigger than the period at the end of a sentence. Over a period of four weeks, it becomes much larger and longer, growing into the worm shape seen in the picture below.

A silkworm making its cocoon.

Interesting Facts about Silkworms

- It takes a silkworm about four days to create its cocoon.

- It takes approximately 3,000 silkworm cocoons to make one meter of silk cloth.

- Although silk is usually used to make clothing, draperies, and upholstery, it is also sometimes used by the manufacturers of some bicycle tires because of its strength.

The next stage in the life of a silkworm is a period of change. The silkworm produces a fine thread and uses it to create a coating that covers its entire body. This covering, called a cocoon, is usually white, cream, or yellow. When the silkworm is ready to make its cocoon, it weighs 10,000 times more than it did when it was an egg. Only one thread is used to make the entire cocoon and this thread can be up to 800 meters* long. The cocoon protects the silkworm while it changes, or transforms, into an insect called a moth. This transformation takes approximately ten days. Once the silkworm comes out of its cocoon as a moth, the female adult moths lay eggs and the process begins all over again.

The threads that weavers use to create silk fabric come from the cocoon itself. In order to make the best silk possible from the cocoon, the threads must not be damaged as the moth comes out. However, if the moth is allowed to leave the cocoon by itself, it will tear most of the threads into small pieces. These can still be used to make silk fabric, but it is not as strong or as beautiful. Unfortunately, to make higher quality fabric, it is necessary to kill the moths before they come out. Then the silk-maker can obtain threads that are very long and very strong. Silk is actually one of the strongest natural materials in the world.

CD 2, Track 10

Word Count: 346
Time: _____

*See page 24 for a metric conversion chart

Vocabulary List

bobbin (14, 15)
craftsman (3, 9, 14, 17)
custom-made (17)
drapery (3, 6)
evolution (9)
fabric (2, 3, 6, 9, 10, 13, 14, 17, 18)
handweave (3, 10, 13, 18)
loom (2, 6, 7, 9, 10, 14, 17)
magnificence (18)
manufacturer (10)
silk (3, 4, 6, 7, 9, 10, 13, 14, 17, 18, 19)
stressful (17)
thread (2, 9, 10, 13, 14, 15)
twist (13, 14)
upholstery (3, 6)
weaver (2, 9)

Metric Conversion Chart

Area
1 hectare = 2.471 acres

Length
1 centimeter = .394 inches
1 meter = 1.094 yards
1 kilometer = .621 miles

Temperature
0° Celsius = 32° Fahrenheit

Volume
1 liter = 1.057 quarts

Weight
1 gram = .035 ounces
1 kilogram = 2.2 pounds